When I Ride in a Car

By Dorothy Chlad

Illustrations by Lydia Halverson

CHILDRENS PRESS, CHICAGO

Library of Congress Cataloging in Publication Data

Chlad, Dorothy.
   When I ride in a car.

   (Safety town)
   Summary: A child describes the safety precautions
her family takes when they go riding in the car.
   1.   Automobiles—Safety measures—Juvenile literature.
2.   Automobiles—Seat belts—Juvenile literature.
[1.   Automobiles—Safety measures.   2.   Automobiles—Seat
belts]   I.   Halverson, Lydia, ill.   II.   Title.
III.   Series: Chlad, Dorothy.   Safety Town.
TL242.C58   1983   629.28'3'0289   83-7382
ISBN O-516-O1987-2

Hi. . . My name is Tommy.

Riding in a car can
be a lot of fun.

Our car takes us on vacations.

We visit grandma
and grandpa, we go to
the shopping mall, the

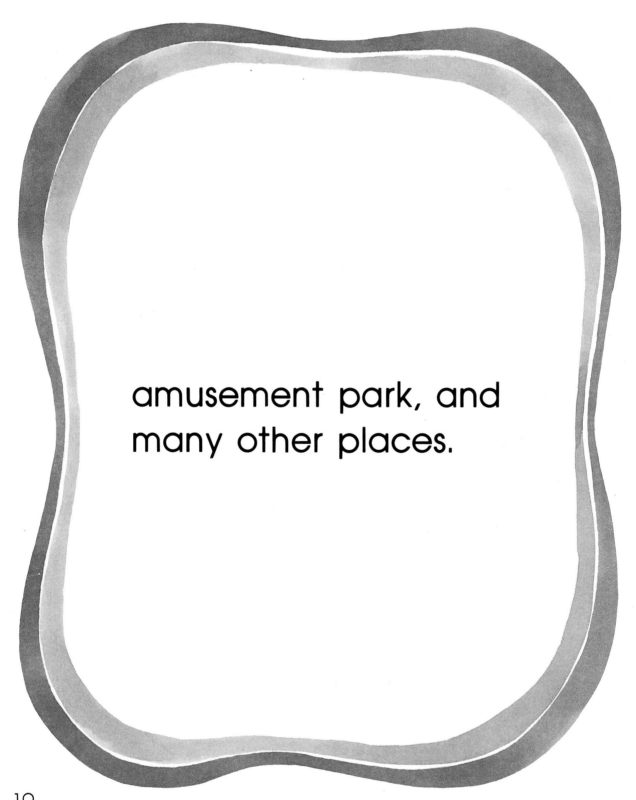

amusement park, and
many other places.

I always buckle my
seat belt. My friends
"buckle-up," too.
This keeps us safe if
the car has to stop
quickly.

13

My little brother sits
in a special car seat.
It keeps him safe.

This picture applies **only** to a car without air bags. If the car has air bags, place the car seat in the rear seat.

15

We never start
driving until everyone is
"buckled-up."

I always ride in the back seat. It is the safest place.

I always talk or play quietly.

The driver must
watch the road and
obey the safety rules.

I can help by not
bothering the driver.

You can be the
driver's helper, too.
Remember my safety
rules. . .

1. Always buckle
your seat belt.

2. Always talk or play quietly.

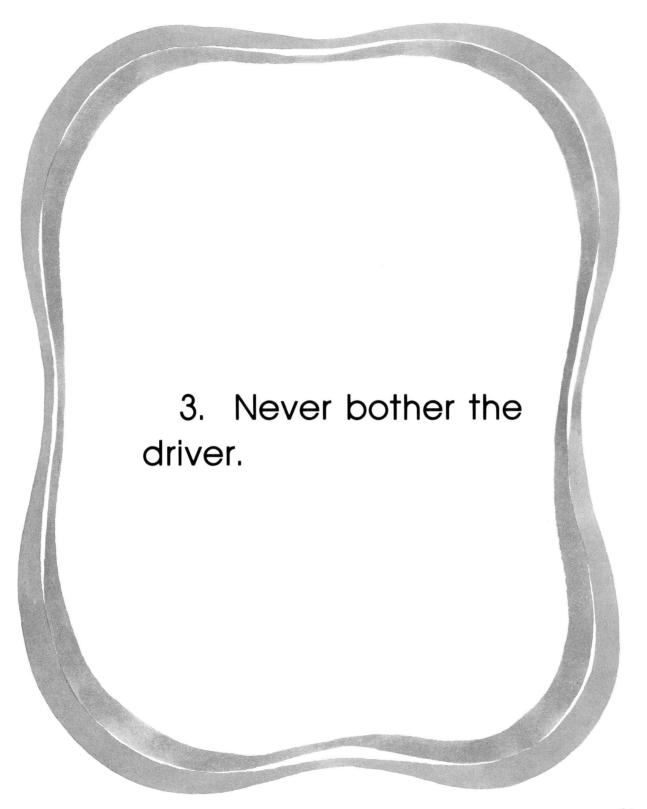

3. Never bother the driver.

About the Author

Dorothy Chlad, founder of the total concept of Safety Town, is recognized internationally as a leader in Preschool/Early Childhood Safety Education. She has authored six books on the program, and has conducted the only workshops dedicated to the concept. Under Mrs. Chlad's direction, the National Safety Town Center was founded; to promote the program through community involvement.

She has presented the importance of safety education at local, state, and national safety and education conferences, such as National Community Education Association, National Safety Council, and the American Driver and Traffic Safety Education Association. She serves as a member of several national committees, such as the Highway Traffic Safety Division and the Educational Resources Division of National Safety Council. Chlad was an active participant at the Sixth International Conference on Safety Education.

Dorothy Chlad continues to serve as a consultant for State Departments of Safety and Education. She has also consulted for the TV program "Sesame Street" and recently wrote this series of safety books for Childrens Press.

A participant of White House Conferences on safety, Dorothy Chlad has received numerous honors and awards including National Volunteer Activist and YMCA Career Woman of Achievement.

About the Artist

Lydia Halverson was born Lydia Geretti in midtown Manhattan. When she was two, her parents left New York and moved to Italy. Four years later her family returned to the United States and settled in the Chicago Area. Lydia attended the University of Illinois, graduating with a degree in fine arts. She worked as a graphic designer for many years before finally concentrating on book illustration.

Lydia lives with her husband and two cats in a suburb of Chicago and is active in several environmental organizations.